THE SOLDIERS ARE COMING!

My Early Life in a Chinese Village

1941 - 1946

Jean Bee Chan

Illustrations by Coral Murakami-Feste.
Book Design by Linda Siegel.

ISBN: 978-17341734-06 (Hardcover)
ISBN: 978-17341734-20 (Paperback)
ISBN: 978-17341734-13 (E-book)

Published by Chan Publishing (jbchanpublishing@gmail.com)
Distributed by Ingram Content Group (ingramcontent.com)
E-book available on Amazon.com

PREFACE

After over forty years of academic life in mathematics, I began to study the Asia Pacific War history, partly because I read the book *The Rape of Nanking* by Iris Chang, and partly because of my mother's sad stories about our hardship in southern China during the war years.

To learn more about the dark history of the atrocities committed against millions of Chinese and other peoples during the Asia Pacific War, I joined several study tours to China and Japan to interview elderly war victims to hear their traumatic experiences first-hand. The victims pleaded with me to tell their stories. One pointed her finger at me, "Tell my story!"

Over the years, I have given public talks describing my own childhood during the Japanese invasion of China. This has always been a painful experience for me, but the audiences found my story touching and meaningful. Finally, it became clear to me that I must put my story in print.

Jean Bee Chan
Marin County, California
October, 2019

DEDICATION

For my late beloved husband Pete, who loved his family dearly and devoted his later life to serving and leading the Rape of Nanking Redress Coalition and the Global Alliance for Preserving the History of World War II in Asia.

THE SOLDIERS ARE COMING!

My Early Life in a Chinese Village

1941 – 1946

Jean Bee Chan

Our family had an idyllic life in Taishan, a small town in southern China. Dad, Mom, my baby brother Datman, and I shared an apartment with my Mom's mother, Popo. Dad worked for the Chinese government and Mom taught in an elementary school.

Popo took care of Datman, and I helped with family chores such as making rice dumplings and sweeping the floor, feeling very grownup at age four. Dad told me once, "You are a good girl."

My parents were very happy to have a son and a daughter, a perfect family. Datman and I were having a

grand time with Popo, playing games, jumping, dancing, and singing together every day.

Then the invading Imperial Japanese forces started bombing Taishan, just a few blocks from our home. Mom and Dad stopped going to work. They talked in whispers, looking worried.

I was scared of the airplane noise and darkened sky. And I couldn't sleep at night.

The bombing continued. The streets of Taishan were filled with frightened folks running for safety, carrying their belongings on their backs.

My own family moved back to the Chan village to live with Grandma, my paternal grandmother.

Meanwhile, Popo returned to live in the Lee village. I hugged her tightly when we said goodbye, and I was sad to see her go.

The first day we arrived at our village, I clutched the new doll Dad bought me to make me feel better about leaving Taishan.

The village kids were fascinated by my doll, and together we walked the doll back and forth in our front yard for hours. By nightfall, my doll was missing, and I was upset for a long time. Mom said in vain, "Your father will buy you another one."

Meanwhile, Dad followed the Chinese government to Chongqing, the wartime capital of China. Dad did not say goodbye to Datman and me; he just left very early one morning while we were still asleep.

I felt abandoned and empty when I realized Dad was no longer with us. Mom later explained, "Chongqing is very far away. Your father was worried that there might not be transportation for us. He may have to walk miles through the mountains. It is safer for us to stay here with Grandma."

But I thought Dad should have taken us with him no matter what.

Our two-story brick house in the village was in the front row of houses facing a small pond and the village well. The house had two apartments, one for Mom and her two kids, the other for Auntie's family.

Between the two apartments was the high ceiling living room for eating and a covered atrium to keep our chickens and pigs. The loft above the living room was for our elders.

We all ate our meals together in the living room, and everyone worked hard to bring food to the table. Life was difficult, but we felt very lucky to be alive.

One of Grandma's chores was to bring enough well water home for drinking, cooking, and washing. I tagged along when Grandma made the daily trip to the well to carry water back to our house. Sometimes, Grandma even let me help her.

I dropped a bucket deep into the well to fill with water, pulled it up to the top of the well, and poured the water into two small buckets. Then I put the buckets on the ends of a bamboo pole and balanced the pole on my shoulders for the short walk home.

Some villagers lingered around the well to share news. Everyone was grateful the bombing did not get to our village.

Dad could not send us letters or money for support, and we didn't hear from him for four whole years because the Japanese soldiers had cut off transportation, mail, food, and medical supplies for our village.

Mom was very resourceful; she quickly learned to cultivate our small plots of land for rice, vegetables, potatoes, and peanuts.

Every day, Grandma and I walked slowly to the fields to water and harvest vegetables. And we went to the mountains to gather dry brush as fuel for cooking.

Grandma was kind and gentle, never in a hurry. We loved each other very much.

Grandma and I also took care of our chickens and pigs. During the daytime, our pigs stayed in the atrium while the chickens scattered in the front lawn to find worms. I was often the one to run around feeding grains to the chickens.

It was my chore to take the family water buffalo to feed on grass fields. One time, when I rode on the buffalo's back toward the river, she waded deep into the water without me. I ran home crying because I was worried that she would drown. Auntie laughed and told me the buffalo could swim.

Then the soldiers began rampaging through the rural villages. They killed everyone in our neighboring village because the villagers tried to protect their livestock.

Whenever the soldiers approached our village, the watchmen would yell, "Soldiers are coming!" We quickly gathered what food and small treasures we had and fled into the mountains. Sometimes we had to stay there all day and all night. The kids played under a fiery sun during the day and huddled together at night.

The soldiers went from house to house, stealing our food and livestock. We lived in daily fear of them.

One afternoon, the soldiers came to our village after a huge storm. We could not reach the mountains because the footbridge leading to the mountains had collapsed the previous night. So we hid in the nearby river behind thick bushes.

By sundown, as high tide came in, I shivered in the cold water and turned blue when the water reached my lips. Mom had been holding my little brother, but Auntie rescued me from drowning by carrying me on her back to keep my head above water. Suddenly two soldiers in green uniforms walked toward the river, pointing their

bayonets at the bushes by the riverbank. We did not dare make any noise for fear of being found.

Luckily the soldiers couldn't see us through the thick bushes; they left after lingering for a long time. We waited quietly for hours until we were sure the soldiers were gone. We were nearly frightened to death.

After returning home, we found our house had been ransacked again. Our pigs and the big urn of rice, intended to feed us for the year, were stolen. All the chickens were scattered and scared.

As the occupation by Japanese soldiers wore on, our rice fields did not produce enough rice to feed us, so Mom sold all her beautiful bridal clothes and jewelry to buy food. She also bought used clothes and sold them for profit away from home.

She was often gone for days at a time. I remember walking around the alleys alone, looking at the grey sky, wondering when my mother would be home again. The next year, Mom found a teaching job in a one-room schoolhouse in another village, a day's walk and a boat ride away.

When Mom went for her teaching job, she left my little brother with Grandma. Mom took me with her because I was old enough for school. We walked a long distance all day and then waited for an overnight boat ride to reach the other village. Upon arrival, Mom and I were housed in a small and lonely schoolhouse.

Mom was paid one bag of rice per student each semester. These bags of rice were riches for us; they kept us from starvation. Mom traded some rice for meat and other necessities.

After a year, Mom could no longer bear the heartache of leaving my brother back home with Grandma. So Mom and I returned to our village. We were alarmed to find Datman very sick from an infection. Gradually Mom nursed him back to health.

As the war years continued, Datman and I grew weaker and weaker from malnutrition and sun exposure. Later, we both ran a fever for days, but we couldn't get any medical treatment since the Japanese soldiers had destroyed all medical clinics.

One night, my brother was extremely uncomfortable and begged Mom for some medicine. She had to tell him she had none to give him. The next afternoon, my brother and I lay in bed, drifting off to sleep. When I awoke, Datman was lifeless, his eyes rolled back into his head. I screamed for my mother. But it was too late. He died later that night, yet another victim of the Japanese invasion of China, among millions of others. My brother was only four years old; I was eight. Mom never forgot she had no medicine to give to her little boy to make him feel better the last night of his short life.

After Datman died, our neighbors came in droves to comfort Mom, and each chided me. "You chased your little brother away." I just stood there in total shock not being able to cry while everyone else wept. I kept wishing I had been the one who died instead. In their grief, Mom and Grandma didn't pay any attention to me. I was abandoned by my brother and everyone else!

Then Popo from the Lee Village came to take me away to live with her. No goodbye from my mother and no explanation why I had to leave her. I stayed at the Lee Village for several months.

I figured Mom didn't want me around anymore. I was sure she didn't love me.

Many years later, I read in Mom's notes that she felt she was a bad mother and it was better for Popo to take care of me. But Mom didn't realize how much I had missed her.

After the Asia Pacific War ended, at the town post office, Mom and I discovered more than one hundred undelivered letters that Dad had sent during our long separation.

In 1946, we were reunited with Dad. Mom told Dad she was deeply ashamed that their son had died of starvation and illness under her care.

My parents later had five more daughters, never able to replace their precious son. And I still have nightmares of the Japanese bombings and the soldiers pointing bayonets at me.

In 1956, my parents and all six daughters immigrated to America to begin a new life in the United States. I am now 82 years old, and I still remember my wartime experience as if it were yesterday.

ABOUT THE AUTHOR

Jean Bee Chan was born in southern China in 1937 when Imperial Japanese forces began bombing China. Later, she went with her mother to live in her ancestral village during the years 1941-46. This book is the true story of her life in that period.

In 1956, her family immigrated to the United States. Chan earned her BS and MS in mathematics from the University of Chicago and her PhD from UCLA. She taught mathematics at Sonoma State University from 1973 to 2015.

Chan co-authored two books: *Discrete Mathematics with Applications*, and *Geometry with Projects and Explorations*. Nationally, she served as governor and vice president of the Mathematical Association of America. In California, Chan co-founded the Asian American Alliance of Marin which promotes justice, tolerance, and networking among Asian Americans. She also co-founded the Asian Scholarship Fund that grants scholarships to deserving high school seniors heading for college. Chan is active in the Rape of Nanking Redress Coalition, based in San Francisco, which seeks justice for the atrocities committed against Chinese and other peoples during the Asia Pacific War.

She was married to her late beloved husband Peter Stanek for 54 years. She now makes her home in Marin County with her loving husband Ken Ross.

She enjoys mathematics, writing, singing, cooking, tai chi, Sudoku, and Chinese brush painting.

ACKNOWLEDGMENTS

I deeply appreciate my family, relatives, friends, and colleagues for encouraging and supporting this writing project.

Sincere thanks to my friends Peter Li and Ying-Ying Chang for support and advice. Special thanks to my husband Ken Ross and my nephew Jesse Wallis for editorial comments.

Most of all, thanks for the love of my children, sisters, husband, and extended family.

CPSIA information can be obtained at www.ICGtesting.com
Printed in the USA
LVIW010314211119
638063LV00002B/8